D1116761

The Wonder of a Waterfall

By Allan Fowler

Consultants

Linda Cornwell, Learning Resource Consultant,
Indiana Department of Education

Sharyn Fenwick, Elementary Science/Math Specialist,
Gustavus Adolphus College, St. Peter, Minnesota

Peter Goodwin, Science Teacher,
Kent School, Kent, Connecticut

Children's Press®
A Division of Grolier Publishing
New York   London   Hong Kong   Sydney
Danbury, Connecticut

Visit Children's Press® on the Internet at:
http://publishing.grolier.com

Designer: Herman Adler Design Group

Library of Congress Cataloging-in-Publication Data

Fowler, Allan.
    The wonder of a waterfall / by Allan Fowler.
      p. cm. – (Rookie read-about science)
    Includes index.
    Summary: Simply describes waterfalls and describes such notable
examples as Niagara Falls and Angel Falls.
    ISBN 0-516-20813-6 (lib.bdg.)   0-516-26483-4 (pbk.)
    1. Waterfalls—Juvenile literature. [1. Waterfalls.] I. Title. II. Series.
GB1403.8.F68   1999   97-31293
551.48'4—dc21   CIP
                               AC

GROLIER
PUBLISHING

Have you ever seen a waterfall?

People often travel far
to see a waterfall.

Who wouldn't like to feel
a waterfall's spray . . .

. . . or hear a waterfall roar as tons and tons of water pour onto the rocks below?

Sometimes the sun
shines on a waterfall's
misty spray and makes
a beautiful rainbow.

Niagara Falls

A waterfall forms where a river or stream spills over a steep cliff.

On the border between the United States and Canada, the Niagara River drops more than 150 feet (46 meters) to form Niagara Falls.

Niagara Falls is made up
of two falls—the American
Falls and the Canadian Falls.

American Falls

Canadian Falls

The Canadian Falls is also called Horseshoe Falls because of its shape. It is wider than the American Falls.

Victoria Falls, in Africa,
is twice as high as Niagara
Falls and much wider.

Iguazú (ee-gwa-SOO) Falls, in South America, is four times wider than Niagara Falls.

The highest waterfall in the world is Angel Falls in Venezuela, South America.

It falls more than half a mile, but it is very narrow.

Few people see Angel Falls, because it lies deep in the rain forest.

15

16

Another very high waterfall is Upper Yosemite Falls.

It can be enjoyed by people who visit Yosemite (yo-SE-me-tee) National Park in California.

The waterfalls we see today
have not always existed.

Niagara Falls formed
about 10,000 years ago.

As the Niagara River
flowed, it wore away the
soft layers of rock below
it. Only the hardest types
of rock remained.

19

The hard rock formed the
cliff that the water spills
over. Many waterfalls
begin this way.

A cliff in a river's path may also be formed by a moving sheet of ice, called a glacier.

As water tumbles over a cliff, it wears away the rock that makes up the cliff.

Every so often, the water loosens a large chunk of rock, and part of the cliff collapses.

Waterfalls are wonderful to see, but they are also useful. In the past, falling water turned waterwheels, which created power to grind grain.

Today, people use the energy
produced by waterfalls to
create electricity. The power
of the water turns turbines
(such as those above).

Would you believe that people have gone over Niagara Falls in a barrel?

The man in this barrel went over in 1945.

The first person to do so was a woman in 1901.

Why would anyone want to
try such a dangerous stunt?

It's enough of a thrill just to watch all that water tumbling over a cliff.

Words You Know

cliff

glacier

rainbow

turbines

waterwheel

30